John Adams

Batter my heart, three-person'd God

Aria from the Opera
Dr. Atomic

for Baritone
Revised Piano Reduction

HENDON MUSIC

BOOSEY & HAWKES

DISTRIBUTED BY

7777 W. BLUEMOUND RD. P.O. BOX 13819 MILWAUKEE, WI 53213

www.boosey.com
www.halleonard.com

Batter my heart, three-person'd God

DOCTOR ATOMIC
Oppenheimer's aria from Act I, Scene 3

Libretto by
PETER SELLARS
drawn from original sources

Music by
JOHN ADAMS
revised piano reduction

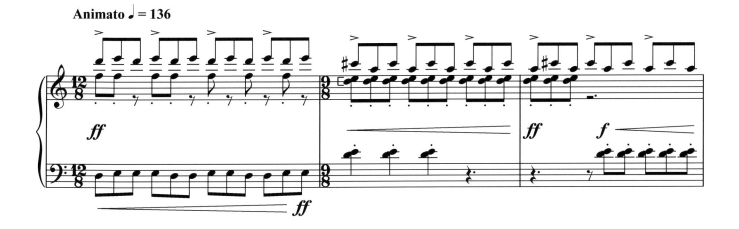

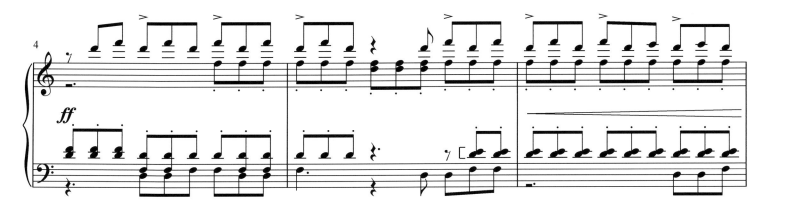

The tempo is deliberately ♩ = 136, not ♩. = 136.

Solennemente

♩ = 58

OPPENHEIMER:

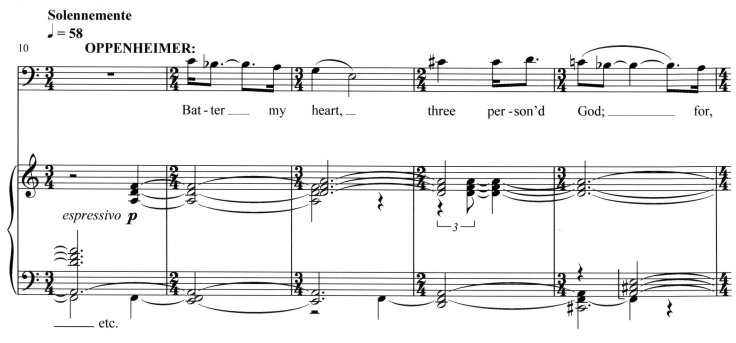

Bat - ter ___ my heart, ___ three per - son'd God; ___ for,

espressivo **p**

___ etc.

you ___ as yet but knock ___ breathe, ___ knock, ___ breath, ___

knock, ___ breath, ___ shine, ___ and ___ seek to mend; ___

mp *espressivo*

8vb

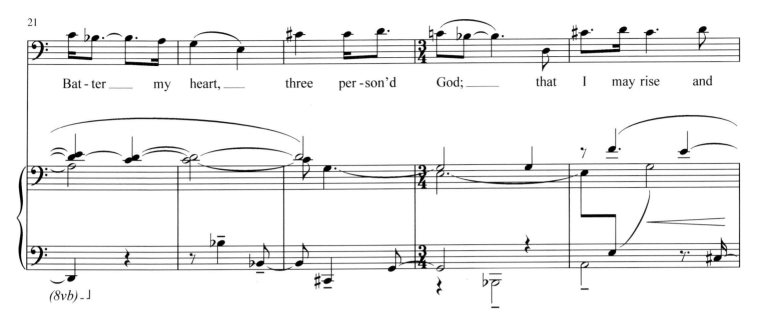

Bat - ter ___ my heart, ___ three per - son'd God; ___ that I may rise and

stand, o -'er - throw ___ me, and bend Your force, ___ to break, ___ blow, ___

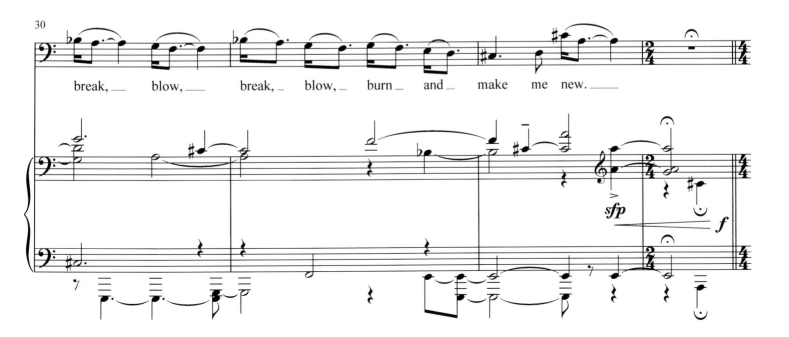

break, ___ blow, ___ break, ___ blow, ___ burn ___ and ___ make me new. ___

6

Animato ♩ = 104

The eighth in measure 1 equals
the new sixteenth note in measure 34.

34

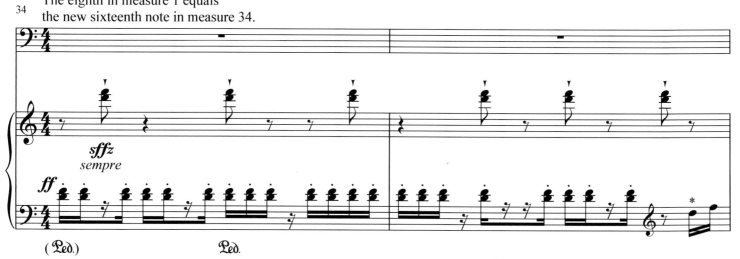

36

38

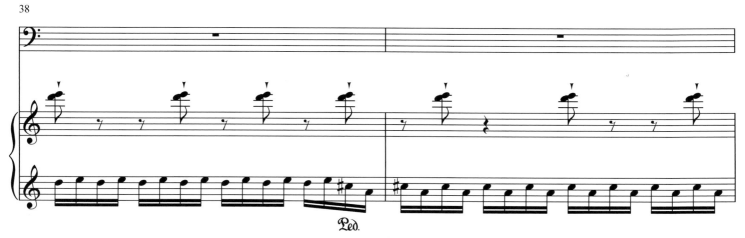

40

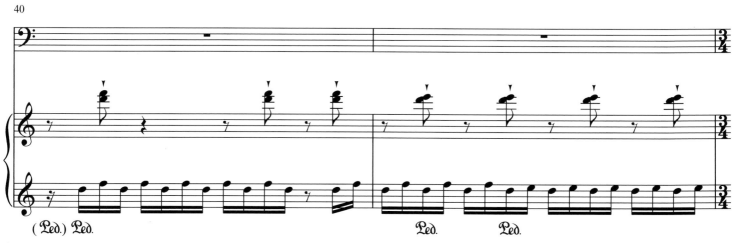

* For fuller sonority, L.H. may play one octave lower through beat one of m. 43.

Slower tempo again

♩ = **58**

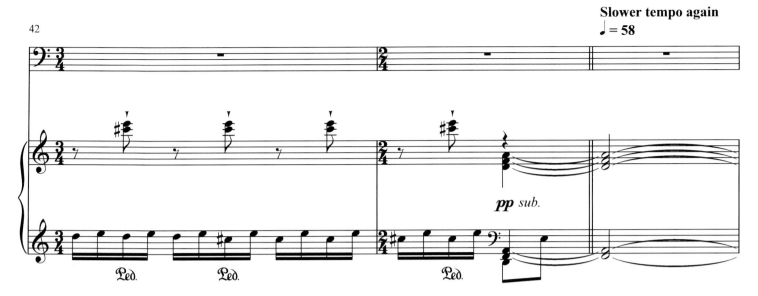

Bat - ter _____ my heart, _____

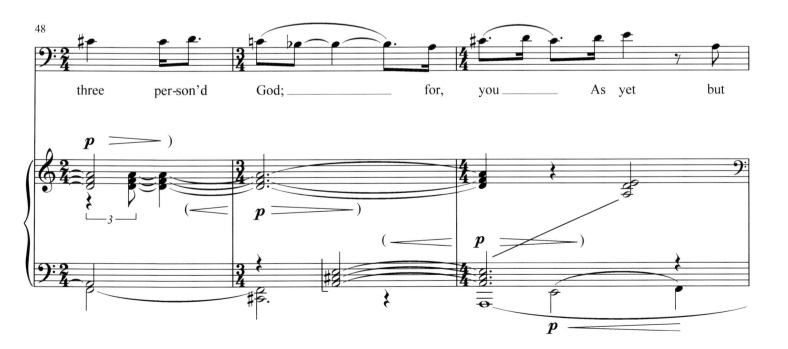

three per-son'd God; _____ for, you _____ As yet but

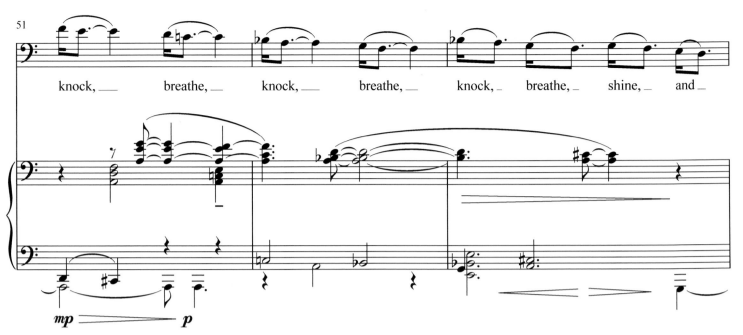

knock, ___ breathe, ___ knock, ___ breathe, ___ knock, ___ breathe, ___ shine, ___ and ___

seek to mend; ___ Bat - ter ___ my heart, ___ three per - son'd

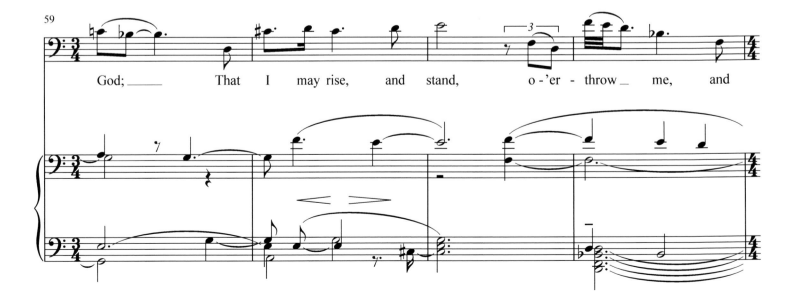

God; ___ That I may rise, and stand, o - 'er - throw ___ me, and

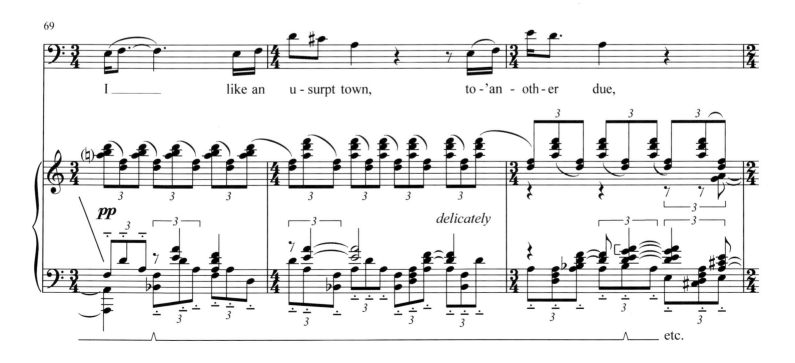

La - bour to'ad -

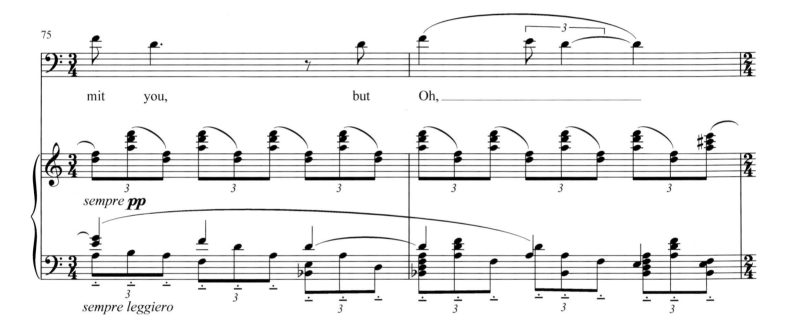

mit you, but Oh,_____

sempre **pp**

sempre leggiero

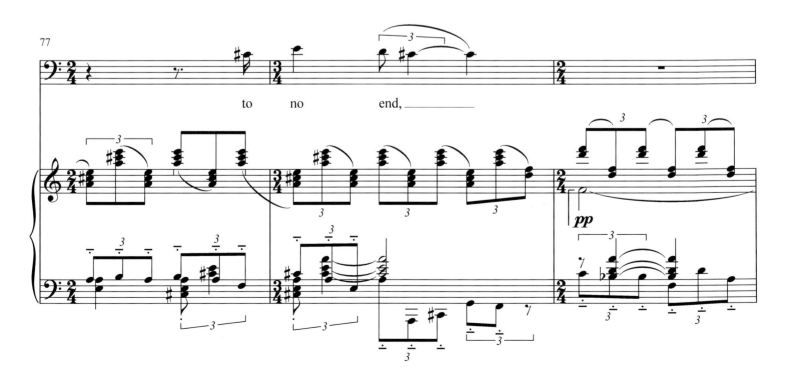

to no end,_____

pp

Rea-son your vice - roy in me,_____ me should de - fend, ___

But is cap - tiv'd, and proves weak_ or un - true, _____

Yet dear - ly'_____ I love you,_____ and would

be_ lov'd fain,_____ But am_ be - troth'd_

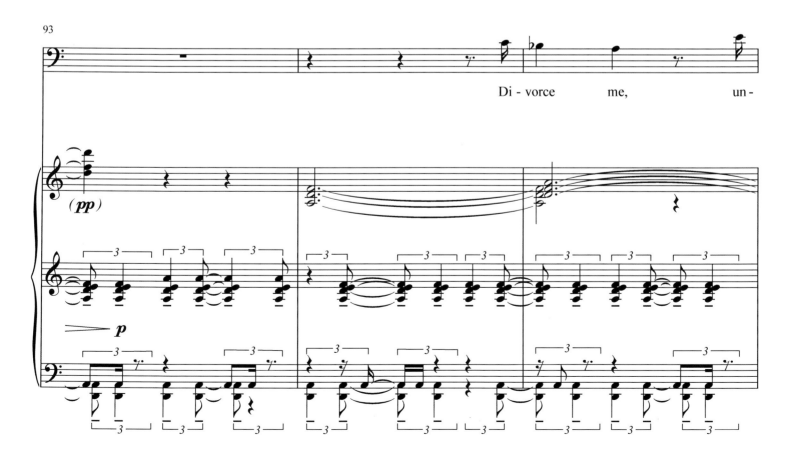

tie, _____ or break that knot a - gain, __

Take me to you, __ im -

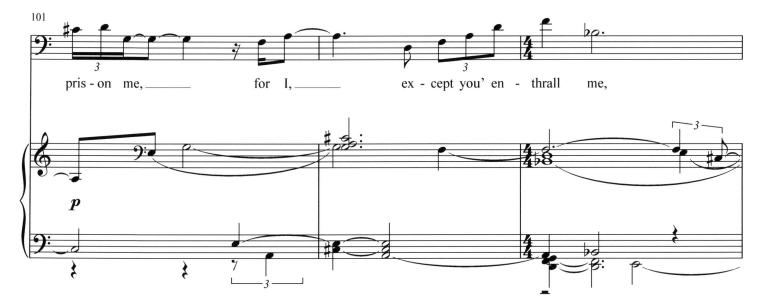

pris - on me, _____ for I, _____ ex - cept you' en - thrall me,

nev - er shall be free, _____ Nor ev - er chaste, _____ ex - cept you _____

ra - vish me. __

BEETHOVEN

PIANO SONATA NO. 24 IN F-SHARP MAJOR

Opus 78

Edited and Recorded by Robert Taub

Also Available:
BEETHOVEN PIANO SONATAS
edited and recorded by Robert Taub

Volume I, Nos. 1–15
00296632 Book only
00296634 CDs only (5 disc set)

Volume II, Nos. 16–32
00296633 Book only
00296635 CDs only (5 disc set)

On the cover:
The Tree of Crows, 1822 (oil on canvas)
by Caspar David Friedrich
(1774–1840)
© Louvre, Paris, France/Giraudon/The Bridgeman Art Library

ISBN 978-1-4768-1633-3

G. SCHIRMER, Inc.

DISTRIBUTED BY

HAL•LEONARD®
CORPORATION
7777 W. BLUEMOUND RD. P.O. BOX 13819 MILWAUKEE, WI 53213

www.schirmer.com
www.halleonard.com

CONTENTS

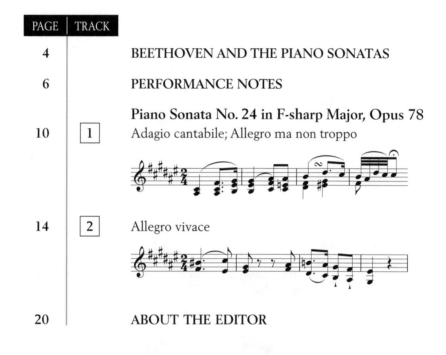

BEETHOVEN
AND THE PIANO SONATAS

In 1816, Beethoven wrote to his friend and admirer Carl Czerny: "You must forgive a composer who would rather hear his work just as he had written it, however beautifully you played it otherwise." Having lost patience with Czerny's excessive interpolations in the piano part of a performance of Beethoven's *Quintet for Piano and Winds*, Op. 16, Beethoven also addressed the envelope sarcastically to "Herr von Zerni, celebrated virtuoso." On all levels, Beethoven meant what he wrote.

As a composer who bridged the gulf between court and private patronage on one hand (the world of Bach, Handel, Haydn, and Mozart) and on the other hand earning a living based substantially on sales of printed works and/or public performances (the world of Brahms), Beethoven was one of the first composers to become almost obsessively concerned with the accuracy of his published scores. He often bemoaned the seeming unending streams of mistakes. "Fehler—fehler!—Sie sind selbst ein einziger Fehler" ("Mistakes—mistakes!—You yourselves are a unique mistake") he wrote to the august publishing firm of Breitkopf und Härtel in 1811.

It is not surprising, therefore, that toward the end of his life Beethoven twice (1822 and again in 1825) begged his publishers C.F. Peters and Schott to bring out a comprehensive complete edition of his works over which Beethoven himself would have editorial control, and would thus be able to ensure accuracy in all dimensions—notes, pedaling and fingering, expressive notations (dynamics, slurs), and articulations, and even movement headings. This never happened.

Beethoven was also obsessive about his musical sketches that he kept with him throughout his mature life. Desk sketchbooks, pocket sketchbooks: thousands of pages reveal his innermost compositional musings, his labored processes of

creativity, the ideas that he abandoned, and the many others—often jumbled together—that he crafted through dint of extraordinary determination, single-minded purpose, and the inspiration of genius into works that endure all exigencies of time and place. In the autograph scores that Beethoven then sent on to publishers, further layers of the creative processes abound. But even these scores might not be the final word in a particular work; there are instances in which Beethoven made textual changes, additions, or deletions by way of letters to publishers, corrections to proofs, and/or post-publication changes to first editions.

We can appreciate the unique qualities of the Beethoven piano sonatas on many different levels. Beethoven's own relationship with these works was fundamentally different from his relationship to his works of other genres. The early sonatas served as vehicles for the young Beethoven as both composer and pianist forging his path in Vienna, the musical capital of Europe at that time. Throughout his compositional lifetime, even when he no longer performed publicly as a pianist, Beethoven used his thirty-two piano sonatas as crucibles for all manner of musical ideas, many of which he later re-crafted—often in a distilled or more rarefied manner—in the sixteen string quartets and the nine symphonies.

The pianoforte was evolving at an enormous rate during the last years of the eighteenth century extending through the first several decades of the nineteenth. As a leading pianist and musical figure of his day, Beethoven was in the vanguard of this technological development. He was not content to confine his often explosive playing to the smaller sonorous capabilities of the instruments he had on hand; similarly, his compositions demanded more from the pianofortes of the day—greater depth of sonority, more subtle levels of keyboard finesse and control, and increased registral range.

These sonatas themselves pushed forward further development and technical innovation from the piano manufacturers.

Motivating many of the sonatas are elements of extraordinary—even revolutionary—musical experimentation extending into domains of form, harmonic development, use of the instrument, and demands placed upon the performer, the piano, and the audience. However, the evolution of these works is not a simple straight line.

I believe that the usual chronological groupings of "early," "middle," and "late" are too superficial for Beethoven's piano sonatas. Since he composed more piano sonatas than substantial works of any other single genre (except songs) and the period of composition of the piano sonatas extends virtually throughout Beethoven's entire creative life, I prefer chronological groupings derived from more specific biographical and stylistic considerations. I delve into greater depth on this and other aspects of the sonatas in my book *Playing the Beethoven Piano Sonatas* (Amadeus Press).

1795–1800: Sonatas Op. 2 no. 1, Op. 2 no. 2, Op. 2 no. 3, Op. 7, Op. 10 no. 1, Op. 10 no. 2, Op. 10 no. 3, Op. 13, Op. 14 no. 1, Op. 14 no. 2, Op. 22, Op. 49 no. 1, Op. 49 no. 2

1800–1802: Sonatas Op. 26, Op. 27 no. 1, Op. 27 no. 2, Op. 28, Op. 31 no. 1, Op. 31 no. 2, Op. 31 no. 3

1804: Sonatas Op. 53, Op. 54, Op. 57

1809: Sonatas Op. 78, Op. 79, Op. 81a

1816–1822: Sonatas Op. 90, Op. 101, Op. 106, Op. 109, Op. 110, Op. 111

From 1804 (post-Heiligenstadt) forward, there were no more multiple sonata opus numbers; each work was assigned its own opus. Beethoven no longer played in public, and his relationship with the sonatas changed subtly.

—*Robert Taub*

PERFORMANCE NOTES

Extracted from *Beethoven: Piano Sonatas Volume II*, edited by Robert Taub.

For the preparation of this edition, I have consulted autograph scores, first editions, and sketchbooks whenever possible. (Complete autograph scores of only twelve of the piano sonatas—plus the autograph of only the first movement of Sonata Op. 81a—have survived.) I have also read Beethoven's letters with particular attention to his many remarks concerning performances of his day and the lists of specific changes/corrections that he sent to publishers. We all know—as did Beethoven—that musical notation is imperfect, but it is the closest representation we have to the artistic ideal of a composer. We strive to represent that ideal as thoroughly and accurately as possible.

Tempo

My recordings of these sonatas are available as companions to the two published volumes. I have also included my suggestions for tempo (metronome markings) for each sonata, at the beginning of each movement.

Fingering

I have included Beethoven's own fingering suggestions. His fingerings—intended not only for himself (in earlier sonatas) but primarily for successive generations of pianists—often reveal intensely musical intentions in their shaping of musical contour and molding of the hands to create specific musical textures. I have added my own fingering suggestions, all of which are aimed at creating meaningful musical constructs. As a general guide, I believe in minimizing hand motions as much as possible, and therefore many of my fingering suggestions are based on the pianist's hands proceeding in a straight line as long as musically viable and physically practicable. I also believe that the pianist can develop senses of tactile feeling for specific musical patterns.

Pedaling

I have also included Beethoven's pedal markings in this edition. These indications are integral parts of the musical fabric. However, since most often no pedal indication is offered, whenever necessary one should use the right pedal—sparingly and subtly—to help achieve legato playing as well as to enhance sonorities.

Ornamentation

My suggestions regarding ornamental turns concern the notion of keeping the contour smooth while providing an expressive musical gesture with an increased sense of forward direction. The actual starting note of a turn depends on the specific context: if it is preceded by the same note (as in Sonata Op. 10 no. 2, second movement, m. 42), then I would suggest that the turn is four notes, starting on the upper neighbor: upper neighbor, main note, lower neighbor, main note.

Sonata in F Major, Opus 10 no. 2:
second movement, m. 42, r.h.

However, if the turn is preceded by another note (as in Sonata Op. 10 no. 2, first movement, m. 38), then the turn could be five notes in total, starting on the main note: main note, upper neighbor, main note, lower neighbor, main note.

Sonata in F Major, Opus 10 no. 2:
first movement, m. 38, r.h.

Whenever Beethoven included an afterbeat (Nachschlag) for a trill, I have included it as well. When he did not, I have not added any.

Footnotes

Footnotes within the musical score offer contextual explanations and alternatives based on earlier representations of the music (first editions, autograph scores) that Beethoven had seen and corrected. In areas where specific markings are visible only in the autograph score, I explain the reasons and context for my choices of musical representation. Other footnotes are intended to clarify ways of playing specific ornaments.

Notes on the Sonata[1]

PIANO SONATA NO. 24 IN F-SHARP MAJOR, OPUS 78 (1809)

Sonata in F-sharp Major, Op. 78, one of Beethoven's favorites, offers subtle glimpses into the future; the concentration on small thematic motives is characteristic of the organic, meticulously composed works of the last period, works in which every nuance is an integral part of the whole. Distinctions between melody and accompaniment begin to dissolve in Op. 78 as thematic motives of equal importance are frequently juxtaposed as counterpoint. The very nature of its closely interrelated themes demands that each be as fully characterized and realized as possible, played so as to distinguish each theme individually but nonetheless to weave them all into a carefully constructed luminescent musical fabric.

The opening figure of the **Allegro ma non troppo** is abstracted throughout the exposition, both melodically and rhythmically. In the development, as the same rhythmic figure forms a counterpoint to the right-hand sixteenth notes, I shape the subtle dynamics of the right hand to mirror the contour of the phrase.

Among the most expressive markings of the first movement is Beethoven's *te-nu-te* (holding back) which he specified in m. 24 (and again in m. 83) for three left-hand chords. I play these three beats at an immediately slower tempo, with a sonorous left hand and articulated right hand so that the first and fourth sixteenth notes of each beat receive a little extra weight. This pattern, of course, is another manifestation of the opening rhythmic cell.

The same dotted rhythm also forms the basis for the first of the two themes of the **Allegro vivace**. However, the rhythmic values are doubled and the metrical position is changed so that the figure begins on the downbeat. The feeling is thus completely different, much more akin to the half-cadence figure first played in mm. 31–32 in the first movement.

Another musical motive in the movement is the grouping of sixteenth notes by twos. The barring of these groups by twos rather than by the more conventional four sixteenth notes—and this is very clear in the autograph score—is a direct indication that Beethoven had in mind detached two-note groups (even though playing four notes in a group is sometimes easier) and that he intended the feelings of breathlessness that this treatment engenders as the second note of each group is detached from the first of the following. The left-hand line therefore should really be as legato as possible, contrasting vividly with the right-hand groups above it and creating a situation of further contrast when the two-note groups alternate between the hands (m. 2 on).

In keeping with the jocundity of this movement, I like to hold the fermatas in mm. 175, 176, and 177 a long time, allowing the surprise to build with each harmony. I then play the final six measures back in tempo, with the left hand as the main line. The rambunctious character of this coda comes in complete contrast to the quiet dignity of the opening Adagio cantabile of the sonata; even though this piece lasts less than eleven minutes, it creates a fully expressive universe.

1 Excerpted from *Playing the Beethoven Piano Sonatas* by Robert Taub
 edited and abridged by Susanne Sheston
 © 2002 by Robert Taub
 Published by Amadeus Press
 Used by permission.

PIANO SONATA NO. 24 IN F-SHARP MAJOR, Opus 78

Dedicated to Countess Therese von Brunswick

Sonata in F-sharp Major

Ludwig van Beethoven
Opus 78
Composed in 1809

Adagio cantabile (♪ = 63)   **Allegro ma non troppo** (♩ = 63)

a) The fingering in italics and the pedal markings are Beethoven's. b) In the autograph and first edition (Breitkopf & Härtel), the *sf* appears as placed (first beat of m. 17) in this edition. Several other editions place this *sf* on the fourth beat of m. 16 in order to be consistent with its placement in the recapitulation (m. 75), also as per the autograph and first edition. (See footnote for m. 75)

c) 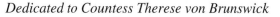 d) Several other editions print the chords in this measure as ⟨notation⟩ in order to be consistent with the F-double sharp in the right hand.

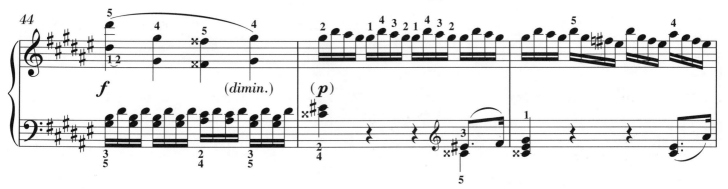

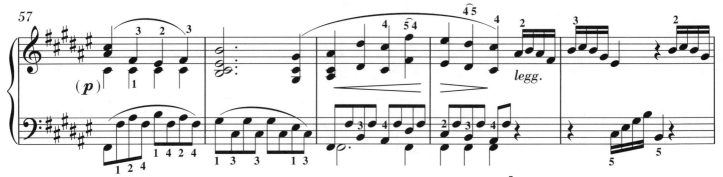

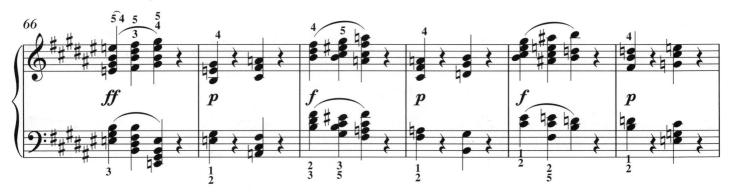

e) See footnote for m. 16. The placement of the *sf* in m. 75 is consistent with the autograph score and first edition. f) See footnote for m. 25. The C-natural in the LH is consistent with the autograph score and first edition. g) *ff* here (compared to *f* in m. 26) as per the autograph.

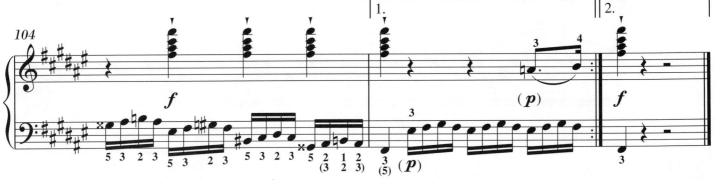

Allegro vivace ($\quarternote$ = 132)

h) Addition of an F-sharp on the fourth beat—as per several other editions, perhaps an attempt at consistency with the second beat—is wrong. The autograph score is clearly notated with the F-sharp–G–E (beats 2, 3, 4) as a separate voice.

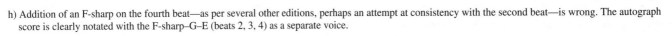

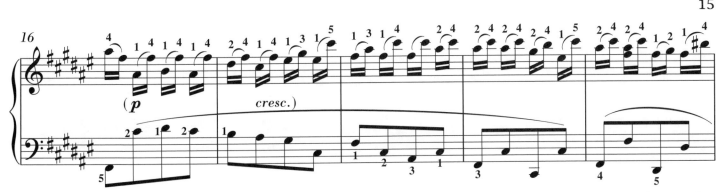

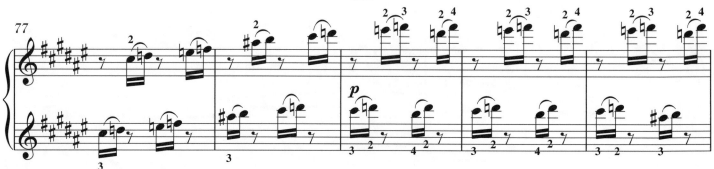

i) LH over RH

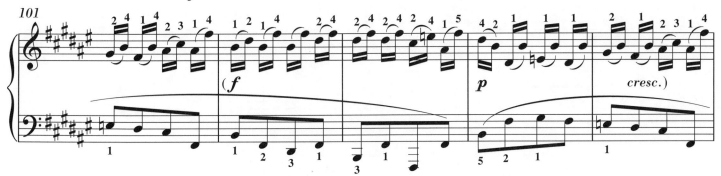

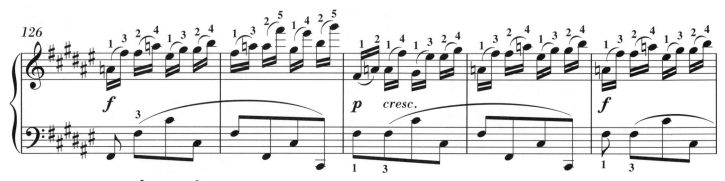

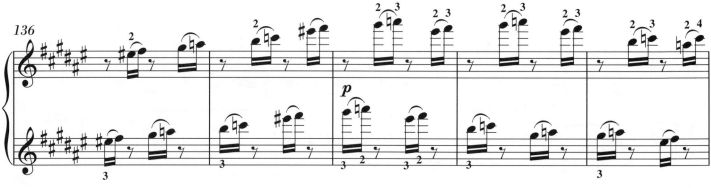

j) The suspension of strict meter in this measure—which is written very broadly by Beethoven in his autograph score—continues and heightens the cadential suspense begun in the previous two measures.

ABOUT THE EDITOR

ROBERT TAUB

From New York's Carnegie Hall to Hong Kong's Cultural Centre to Germany's *avant garde* Zentrum für Kunst und Medientechnologie, Robert Taub is acclaimed internationally. He has performed as soloist with the MET Orchestra in Carnegie Hall, the Boston Symphony Orchestra, BBC Philharmonic, The Philadelphia Orchestra, San Francisco Symphony, Los Angeles Philharmonic, Montreal Symphony, Munich Philharmonic, Orchestra of St. Luke's, Hong Kong Philharmonic, Singapore Symphony, and others.

Robert Taub has performed solo recitals on the Great Performers Series at New York's Lincoln Center and other major series worldwide. He has been featured in international festivals, including the Saratoga Festival, the Lichfield Festival in England, San Francisco's Midsummer Mozart Festival, the Geneva International Summer Festival, among others.

Following the conclusion of his highly celebrated New York series of Beethoven Piano Sonatas, Taub completed a sold-out Beethoven cycle in London at Hampton Court Palace. His recordings of the complete Beethoven Piano Sonatas have been praised throughout the world for their insight, freshness, and emotional involvement. In addition to performing, Robert Taub is an eloquent spokesman for music, giving frequent engaging and informal lectures and pre-concert talks. His book on Beethoven—*Playing the Beethoven Piano Sonatas*—has been published internationally by Amadeus Press.

Taub was featured in a recent PBS television program—*Big Ideas*—that highlighted him playing and discussing Beethoven Piano Sonatas. Filmed during his time as Artist-in-Residence at the Institute for Advanced Study, this program has been broadcast throughout the US on PBS affiliates.

Robert Taub's performances are frequently broadcast on radio networks around the world, including the NPR (Performance Today), Ireland's RTE, and Hong Kong's RTHK. He has also recorded the Sonatas of Scriabin and works of Beethoven, Schumann, Liszt, and Babbitt for Harmonia Mundi, several of which have been selected as "critic's favorites" by *Gramophone*, *Newsweek*, *The New York Times*, *The Washington Post*, *Ovation*, and *Fanfare*.

Robert Taub is involved with contemporary music as well as the established literature, premiering piano concertos by Milton Babbitt (MET Orchestra, James Levine) and Mel Powell (Los Angeles Philharmonic), and making the first recordings of the Persichetti Piano Concerto (Philadelphia Orchestra, Charles Dutoit) and Sessions Piano Concerto. He has premiered six works of Milton Babbitt (solo piano, chamber music, Second Piano Concerto). Taub has also collaborated with several 21st-century composers, including Jonathan Dawe (USA), David Bessell (UK), and Ludger Brümmer (Germany) performing their works in America and Europe.

Taub is a Phi Beta Kappa graduate of Princeton where he was a University Scholar. As a Danforth Fellow he completed his doctoral degree at The Juilliard School where he received the highest award in piano. Taub has served as Artist-in-Residence at Harvard University, at UC Davis, as well as at the Institute for Advanced Study. He has led music forums at Oxford and Cambridge Universities and The Juilliard School. Taub has also been Visiting Professor at Princeton University and at Kingston University (UK).